Breaking Free

Escaping Toxic Relationships with Family, Friends, and Partners

By Jalyn Jace

BREAKING FREE

First edition. April 25, 2024.

Copyright © 2024 jalyn jace.

ISBN: 979-8224186440

Written by jalyn jace.

Table of Contents

Chapter 1: Recognizing Toxic Relationships

Recognizing Signs of Toxicity in Relationships

Toxicity in relationships can manifest in various forms, impacting our mental, emotional, and physical well-being. In this chapter, we'll explore the common signs of toxicity in family dynamics, friendships, and romantic partnerships, empowering you to identify red flags and take steps to protect your overall health and happiness.

Signs of Toxicity in Family Dynamics:

1. Control and Manipulation: Toxic family dynamics often involve controlling behavior, where one or more members exert power over others through manipulation, guilt-tripping, or coercion.

2. Lack of Boundaries: Healthy families respect individual boundaries and autonomy. In toxic families, boundaries may be disregarded or violated, leading to feelings of intrusion and disrespect.

3. Emotional Neglect: Emotional neglect occurs when family members fail to meet each other's emotional needs, leading to feelings of loneliness, invalidation, and low self-worth.

4. Enmeshment: Enmeshment refers to unhealthy emotional boundaries within the family, where individual identities become blurred, and members have difficulty distinguishing their own thoughts, feelings, and desires from those of others.

5. Dysfunctional Communication: Toxic families may struggle with communication patterns characterized by criticism, blame, and avoidance, making it difficult to resolve conflicts and express emotions in a healthy manner.

Signs of Toxicity in Friendships:

1. Manipulative Behavior: Toxic friends may use manipulation tactics to control or influence your thoughts, emotions, and actions, often leaving you feeling confused, guilty, or obligated.

2. One-Sided Relationships: Healthy friendships are built on mutual respect and reciprocity. In toxic friendships, one person may consistently prioritize their own needs and desires, neglecting or disregarding yours.

3. Constant Criticism: Toxic friends may criticize or belittle you, undermining your self-esteem and confidence over time. Criticism disguised as "constructive feedback" can still be harmful if it erodes your sense of self-worth.

4. Jealousy and Competition: Toxic friends may feel threatened by your successes or accomplishments, leading to jealousy and competitiveness. They may undermine your achievements or seek to outshine you to boost their own ego.

5. Lack of Support: Friends are meant to support and uplift each other through life's challenges. In toxic friendships, you may find that your friend is unsupportive, dismissive, or indifferent to your struggles and successes.

Signs of Toxicity in Romantic Partnerships:

1. Control and Possessiveness: Toxic partners may exhibit controlling behavior, such as monitoring your activities, isolating you from friends and family, or dictating your choices and decisions.

2. Emotional Abuse: Emotional abuse can take many forms, including verbal attacks, manipulation, gaslighting, and threats. It undermines your self-esteem and emotional well-being, leaving you feeling trapped and powerless.

3. Lack of Respect for Boundaries: Healthy relationships respect individual boundaries and autonomy. In toxic partnerships, boundaries may be disregarded or violated, leading to feelings of invasion and violation.

4. Power Imbalance: Toxic relationships often involve a power imbalance, where one partner holds more control or influence over the other. This can lead to feelings of disempowerment and dependence.

5. Unresolved Conflict: Healthy relationships navigate conflicts constructively, with both partners actively seeking resolution and understanding. In toxic relationships, conflicts may escalate or remain unresolved, leading to ongoing tension and resentment.

Understanding the signs of toxicity in relationships is essential in protecting your mental, emotional, and physical well-being. By recognizing red flags in family dynamics, friendships, and romantic partnerships, you can take proactive steps to set boundaries, prioritize self-care, and cultivate healthier, more fulfilling connections in your life. Remember, you deserve relationships that uplift and support you, and it's okay to distance yourself from those that undermine your happiness and growth.

Exploring the Impact of Toxic Relationships

Toxic relationships can have profound effects on our mental, emotional, and physical well-being, often leaving lasting scars that require time and effort to heal. In this chapter, we'll delve into the complex ways in which toxic relationships can impact us, shedding light on the emotional, psychological, and physical consequences that may arise from prolonged exposure to toxicity.

Emotional Impact:

1. Erosion of Self-Esteem: Toxic relationships can chip away at our self-esteem, leaving us feeling unworthy, inadequate, and undeserving of love and respect.

2. Increased Anxiety and Stress: Constant exposure to toxicity can lead to heightened levels of anxiety and stress, as we navigate unpredictable behavior, emotional manipulation, and conflict.

3. Emotional Exhaustion: Toxic relationships can be emotionally draining, leaving us feeling exhausted, depleted, and emotionally overwhelmed.

4. Feelings of Isolation and Loneliness: Despite being in a relationship, toxic dynamics can lead to feelings of isolation and loneliness, as we struggle to connect with others authentically and feel understood and supported.

5. Trust Issues: Toxic relationships can erode our trust in others, making it difficult to form meaningful connections and establish healthy boundaries in future relationships.

Psychological Impact:

1. Gaslighting and Manipulation: Gaslighting and manipulation tactics used in toxic relationships can lead to confusion, self-doubt, and a distorted sense of reality.

2. Anxiety Disorders: Prolonged exposure to toxicity can contribute to the development of anxiety disorders, including generalized anxiety disorder (GAD), panic disorder, and social anxiety disorder.

3. Depression: Toxic relationships can exacerbate feelings of sadness, hopelessness, and despair, contributing to the onset or worsening of depression.

4. Post-Traumatic Stress Disorder (PTSD): Traumatic experiences within toxic relationships, such as emotional abuse or physical violence, can lead to the development of PTSD, characterized by intrusive memories, flashbacks, and hypervigilance.

5. Negative Self-Talk: Toxic relationships can foster negative self-talk and self-criticism, as we internalize the hurtful messages and beliefs perpetuated by the toxic individual.

Physical Impact:

1. Sleep Disturbances: Toxic relationships can disrupt sleep patterns, leading to insomnia, nightmares, and other sleep disturbances.

2. Physical Symptoms: Prolonged stress and anxiety associated with toxic relationships can manifest in physical symptoms, such as headaches, digestive issues, and muscle tension.

3. Weakened Immune System: Chronic stress and emotional turmoil can weaken the immune system, making us more susceptible to illness and infection.

4. Substance Abuse: Coping with the pain and stress of a toxic relationship may lead some individuals to turn to substance abuse as a way to self-medicate and numb their emotions.

5. Long-Term Health Consequences: The cumulative effects of toxic relationships can contribute to long-term health consequences, including cardiovascular disease, autoimmune disorders, and chronic pain conditions.

Toxic relationships can have far-reaching effects on our mental, emotional, and physical health, impacting every aspect of our lives. By understanding the emotional, psychological, and physical consequences of toxicity, we can take proactive steps to protect ourselves and prioritize our well-being. Remember, you deserve relationships that uplift and support you, and it's okay to distance yourself from those that undermine your happiness and growth. Healing from the wounds of toxicity may take time, but with self-compassion, support, and resilience, it is possible to reclaim your sense of self and build a life filled with love, joy, and fulfillment.

Confronting Toxic Behavior: Navigating Fear and Resistance

Confronting toxic behavior within relationships is a daunting task that often evokes feelings of fear, uncertainty, and resistance. In this chapter, we'll explore the challenges of acknowledging toxic behavior and overcoming the fear of change, offering insights and strategies to help you navigate this difficult process with courage and resilience.

Acknowledging the Reality of Toxic Behavior:

1. Denial and Minimization: It's common to deny or minimize the extent of toxic behavior within relationships, especially if we have invested time, energy, and emotions into maintaining them.

2. Rationalization and Justification: We may rationalize or justify toxic behavior, attributing it to external circumstances or convincing ourselves that it's temporary and manageable.

3. Shame and Guilt: Feelings of shame and guilt can arise when acknowledging toxic behavior within ourselves or others, leading to avoidance and denial as coping mechanisms.

4. Fear of Confrontation: The prospect of confronting toxic behavior can be intimidating, triggering fear of conflict, rejection, or retaliation from the toxic individual.

5. Hope for Change: Despite the toxicity, we may hold onto hope that the individual will change their behavior, leading us to tolerate

or enable toxic patterns out of a desire for reconciliation or redemption.

Understanding the Fear of Change:

1. Fear of the Unknown: Change represents uncertainty and unpredictability, triggering fear of the unknown and apprehension about what lies ahead.

2. Comfort in Familiarity: Toxic relationships, despite their harmful dynamics, offer a sense of familiarity and security, making it difficult to envision a life without them.

3. Loss and Grief: Confronting toxic behavior entails letting go of relationships, patterns, and identities that may have defined us for years, leading to feelings of loss and grief.

4. Fear of Abandonment: Confronting toxic behavior may result in rejection or abandonment from the toxic individual or others within the relationship's orbit, intensifying fear and resistance.

5. Self-Doubt and Insecurity: Fear of change may stem from self-doubt and insecurity, as we question our ability to navigate uncertainty and cope with the challenges of transformation.

Navigating Fear and Resistance:

1. Cultivate Self-Compassion: Practice self-compassion as you navigate the complexities of confronting toxic behavior, acknowledging that change is a process filled with ups and downs.

2. Seek Support: Surround yourself with supportive friends, family members, or mental health professionals who can offer

encouragement, guidance, and validation as you confront toxicity and embrace change.

3. Set Boundaries: Establish clear boundaries to protect your emotional and mental well-being as you navigate confrontations with toxic behavior. Communicate your boundaries assertively and enforce them consistently.

4. Practice Self-Care: Prioritize self-care practices that nourish your mind, body, and soul, providing you with the strength and resilience to confront toxic behavior and navigate the fear of change.

5. Embrace Growth Mindset: Embrace a growth mindset that views challenges and setbacks as opportunities for learning and growth, empowering you to confront toxic behavior with courage and resilience.

Confronting toxic behavior within relationships requires courage, resilience, and self-compassion. By acknowledging the difficulty of confronting toxicity and navigating the fear of change, you can empower yourself to embrace transformation and cultivate healthier, more fulfilling relationships. Remember, change is a process, and it's okay to seek support, set boundaries, and prioritize self-care as you navigate the complexities of confronting toxicity and embracing growth.

Chapter 2: Unraveling Family Dynamics

Navigating Toxic Family Dynamics: Understanding Intergenerational Patterns

Toxic family relationships can be deeply entrenched, shaped by intergenerational patterns and dynamics that influence behavior, communication, and relationships. In this chapter, we'll explore the complexities of toxic family dynamics and the role of intergenerational patterns in perpetuating harmful behaviors, offering insights and strategies to help you navigate these challenging relationships with awareness and resilience.

Understanding Intergenerational Patterns:

1. Family Systems Theory: Family systems theory posits that families operate as interconnected units, with each member influencing and being influenced by others. Intergenerational patterns are passed down through generations, shaping family dynamics and behaviors.

2. Learned Behaviors: Children learn how to interact and communicate within the family unit by observing and emulating the behaviors of their parents and caregivers. Toxic behaviors and coping mechanisms may be passed down unconsciously, perpetuating harmful patterns.

3. Role Modeling: Parents serve as primary role models for their children, modeling interpersonal skills, coping strategies, and conflict resolution techniques. Children may internalize and

replicate these behaviors in their own relationships, perpetuating intergenerational patterns of toxicity.

4. Unresolved Trauma: Traumatic experiences within the family, such as abuse, neglect, addiction, or mental illness, can leave lasting scars that reverberate through generations. Unresolved trauma may manifest in dysfunctional coping mechanisms and maladaptive behaviors that perpetuate toxicity.

5. Cultural and Societal Influences: Cultural and societal norms shape family dynamics and expectations, influencing attitudes towards power, authority, gender roles, and emotional expression. These influences can either perpetuate or challenge intergenerational patterns of toxicity within families.

Examining Complexities of Toxic Family Dynamics:

1. Power Dynamics: Toxic family dynamics often involve imbalances of power and control, where certain members exert authority or dominance over others through manipulation, coercion, or emotional abuse.

2. Enmeshment and Boundaries: Enmeshment refers to blurred or nonexistent boundaries within the family unit, where individual identities become intertwined, and personal autonomy is compromised. Establishing healthy boundaries is essential in navigating toxic family dynamics and protecting individual well-being.

3. Communication Patterns: Communication styles within toxic families may be characterized by criticism, blame, defensiveness, and

avoidance, making it difficult to express emotions, resolve conflicts, and foster genuine connection.

4. Triangulation: Triangulation occurs when conflicts or tensions within the family are redirected or projected onto a third party, creating alliances and divisions that further destabilize family dynamics.

5. Guilt and Obligation: Toxic family dynamics often perpetuate feelings of guilt, obligation, and duty, leading individuals to prioritize family harmony at the expense of their own well-being and autonomy.

Navigating Intergenerational Patterns:

1. Self-Reflection: Take time to reflect on your own experiences within the family and identify patterns of behavior, communication, and coping mechanisms that may have been influenced by intergenerational dynamics.

2. Seek Therapy: Consider seeking the guidance of a therapist or counselor who can help you explore and process intergenerational patterns, trauma, and unresolved conflicts within the family.

3. Set Boundaries: Establish clear boundaries to protect your emotional and mental well-being within toxic family dynamics. Communicate your boundaries assertively and enforce them consistently.

4. Break the Cycle: Recognize your power to break the cycle of toxicity within your family by fostering healthy relationships, communication, and coping strategies. Be a role model for future generations by promoting empathy, compassion, and authenticity.

5. Cultivate Supportive Networks: Surround yourself with supportive friends, chosen family members, or support groups who validate your experiences and offer unconditional support as you navigate toxic family dynamics.

Navigating toxic family dynamics and intergenerational patterns requires courage, self-awareness, and resilience. By examining the complexities of toxic family relationships and understanding the role of intergenerational patterns, you can empower yourself to break free from harmful cycles and cultivate healthier, more fulfilling relationships. Remember, you have the power to rewrite your family narrative and create a legacy of healing and growth for future generations.

The Legacy of Childhood: Impact on Adult Relationships

Our childhood experiences shape the foundation of who we are and how we navigate the world, including our relationships with others. In this chapter, we'll explore the profound impact of childhood experiences on adult relationships, examining how early attachments, traumas, and patterns influence our behavior, communication, and emotional well-being in intimate, familial, and social connections.

Attachment Theory:

1. Secure Attachment: Children who experience secure attachment with caregivers develop a sense of trust, safety, and emotional security. As adults, they are more likely to form stable, supportive relationships characterized by intimacy, mutual respect, and effective communication.

2. Insecure Attachment: Insecure attachment styles, such as anxious-preoccupied, dismissive-avoidant, and fearful-avoidant, stem from inconsistent or inadequate caregiving in childhood. These attachment patterns can manifest in adult relationships as difficulty with intimacy, fear of abandonment, and challenges in regulating emotions and forming healthy attachments.

Impact of Childhood Trauma:

1. Adverse Childhood Experiences (ACEs): Adverse childhood experiences, such as abuse, neglect, family dysfunction, and parental substance abuse, can have lasting effects on mental, emotional, and physical health. ACEs increase the risk of psychological disorders, substance abuse, and interpersonal difficulties in adulthood.

2. Complex Trauma: Complex trauma refers to prolonged or repeated exposure to traumatic events, often within the family system. Complex trauma can impair attachment, emotion regulation, and interpersonal skills, making it challenging to form and maintain healthy relationships in adulthood.

Learned Relationship Patterns:

1. Modeling Behavior: Children learn how to navigate relationships by observing and internalizing the behaviors of their caregivers. Positive role modeling promotes healthy relationship skills, while negative modeling can perpetuate dysfunctional patterns and behaviors.

2. Interpersonal Scripts: Interpersonal scripts are unconscious patterns of behavior, communication, and interaction learned in childhood. These scripts influence how we approach conflict, express emotions, and form attachments in adult relationships.

Emotional Regulation and Coping Mechanisms:

1. Emotional Regulation: Childhood experiences shape our ability to regulate emotions and cope with stress. Children who learn effective emotion regulation strategies are better equipped to navigate conflicts and challenges in adult relationships.

2. Maladaptive Coping Mechanisms: In response to childhood trauma or adversity, individuals may develop maladaptive coping mechanisms, such as avoidance, numbing, or aggression, which can undermine healthy relationships and perpetuate cycles of dysfunction.

Breaking the Cycle:

1. Self-Awareness: Cultivate self-awareness by reflecting on your childhood experiences, attachment patterns, and relationship dynamics. Recognize how past experiences may influence your behavior, beliefs, and expectations in adult relationships.

2. Healing Trauma: Seek support from therapists, counselors, or support groups to process and heal from childhood trauma and adverse experiences. Trauma-informed therapy can help you develop coping strategies, regulate emotions, and form healthy attachments.

3. Rewriting the Narrative: Challenge negative beliefs and scripts learned in childhood by consciously choosing to rewrite your relationship narrative. Practice self-compassion, forgiveness, and empathy towards yourself and others as you navigate the complexities of adult relationships.

4. Cultivating Healthy Relationships: Invest in building healthy, fulfilling relationships characterized by trust, communication, and mutual respect. Surround yourself with supportive individuals who validate your experiences and encourage your growth and healing.

Childhood experiences profoundly shape our adult relationships, influencing our attachment patterns, emotional regulation, and interpersonal dynamics. By understanding the impact of childhood experiences on adult relationships and actively working towards healing and growth, we can break free from harmful cycles, cultivate healthy connections, and create a future filled with love, resilience, and fulfillment. Remember, you have the power to rewrite your relationship narrative and build the nurturing, supportive connections you deserve.

Balancing Guilt and Self-Care in Family Relationships

Navigating guilt and obligation within family dynamics can be a delicate balancing act, especially when prioritizing self-care. In this chapter, we'll explore the complexities of guilt and obligation in family relationships and offer strategies to help you prioritize your well-being while maintaining healthy connections with your loved ones.

Understanding Guilt and Obligation:

1. Familial Expectations: Family dynamics often come with a set of expectations and obligations rooted in tradition, culture, and upbringing. These expectations can exert pressure to conform and prioritize familial needs above your own.

2. Emotional Manipulation: Guilt may be used as a tool for emotional manipulation within family relationships, coercing individuals into compliance or sacrificing their own needs and desires to fulfill familial expectations.

3. Cultural and Societal Norms: Cultural and societal norms may reinforce the idea that family loyalty and obligation are paramount, making it challenging to assert boundaries and prioritize self-care without feeling guilty or selfish.

Challenges of Prioritizing Self-Care:

1. Fear of Rejection: Prioritizing self-care may evoke fear of rejection or abandonment from family members who perceive it as a betrayal of familial duties or expectations.

2. Internalized Guilt: Individuals may internalize feelings of guilt for prioritizing their own well-being over the needs of their family, leading to self-doubt, shame, and anxiety.

3. Boundary Setting: Establishing boundaries to protect your emotional and mental well-being within family dynamics can be met with resistance or pushback, exacerbating feelings of guilt and obligation.

Strategies for Balancing Guilt and Self-Care:

1. Practice Self-Compassion: Recognize that prioritizing self-care is not selfish but essential for your overall well-being. Practice self-compassion by treating yourself with kindness and understanding as you navigate feelings of guilt and obligation.

2. Communicate Openly: Communicate your needs, boundaries, and intentions with honesty and transparency to your family members. Clearly articulate why self-care is important to you and how it benefits both yourself and your relationships.

3. Set Boundaries: Establish clear boundaries to protect your emotional and mental health within family relationships. Communicate your boundaries assertively and enforce them consistently, even if it means saying no to certain requests or obligations.

4. Seek Support: Surround yourself with supportive friends, chosen family members, or mental health professionals who validate your

experiences and offer encouragement as you navigate guilt and self-care within family dynamics.

5. Reevaluate Expectations: Reflect on and challenge familial expectations and obligations that may be rooted in guilt or manipulation. Question whether these expectations align with your values, priorities, and well-being, and adjust accordingly.

Balancing guilt and self-care within family relationships is a challenging but necessary endeavor for maintaining emotional and mental well-being. By understanding the complexities of guilt and obligation, practicing self-compassion, setting boundaries, and seeking support, you can navigate family dynamics with greater resilience and authenticity. Remember, prioritizing self-care is not selfish but essential for creating healthy, fulfilling relationships rooted in mutual respect and understanding.

Chapter 3: Toxic Friendships: Recognizing Red Flags

Recognizing Toxic Behaviors in Friendships

Friendships are meant to be sources of support, understanding, and joy. However, not all friendships are healthy, and toxic behaviors can erode trust and cause harm. In this chapter, we'll delve into the signs of toxicity in friendships, including manipulation, betrayal, and emotional manipulation, empowering you to identify red flags and protect your well-being.

Manipulation:

1. Gaslighting: Gaslighting is a form of manipulation where a friend distorts facts, denies reality, or undermines your perceptions to make you doubt your own sanity or judgment.

2. Guilt-Tripping: Toxic friends may use guilt as a tool for manipulation, making you feel responsible for their emotions or choices and coercing you into doing things you're uncomfortable with.

3. Emotional Blackmail: Emotional blackmail involves using threats, manipulation, or emotional manipulation to control your actions or behavior, often by threatening to end the friendship or withdraw affection.

Betrayal:

1. Disloyalty: Betrayal can take many forms, including sharing confidences with others, spreading rumors or gossip, or undermining your trust by lying or deceit.

2. Lack of Respect for Boundaries: Toxic friends may disregard your boundaries or violate your trust, leaving you feeling betrayed and vulnerable.

3. Self-Interest: Betrayal often stems from self-interest, where a friend prioritizes their own needs, desires, or agenda over your well-being, feelings, or trust.

Emotional Manipulation:

1. Invalidating Your Feelings: Toxic friends may invalidate your feelings or experiences, minimizing your emotions or dismissing your concerns, which can lead to self-doubt and confusion.

2. Playing the Victim: Emotional manipulation may involve playing the victim to garner sympathy, attention, or support, making you feel guilty or responsible for their well-being.

3. Passive-Aggressive Behavior: Passive-aggressive behavior is a form of emotional manipulation characterized by indirect communication, sarcasm, or subtle insults that undermine your confidence and self-esteem.

Identifying Red Flags:

1. Inconsistency: Toxic friendships may be marked by inconsistency, where your friend's behavior or attitude fluctuates unpredictably, leaving you feeling confused or insecure.

2. Lack of Empathy: Empathy is a cornerstone of healthy friendships, but toxic friends may lack empathy or understanding for your feelings, needs, or experiences.

3. Power Imbalance: Toxic friendships often involve a power imbalance, where one friend holds more control or influence over the other, leading to feelings of dependence or inadequacy.

Protecting Your Well-Being:

1. Trust Your Instincts: Pay attention to your instincts and feelings about the friendship. If something feels off or uncomfortable, it's important to trust yourself and take action to protect your well-being.

2. Set Boundaries: Establish clear boundaries to protect yourself from manipulation, betrayal, or emotional manipulation. Communicate your boundaries assertively and enforce them consistently.

3. Seek Support: Don't hesitate to seek support from trusted friends, family members, or mental health professionals if you're struggling with a toxic friendship. Surround yourself with individuals who validate your experiences and offer unconditional support.

Conclusion:

Recognizing toxic behaviors in friendships is essential for protecting your well-being and cultivating healthy, fulfilling relationships. By identifying red flags such as manipulation, betrayal, and emotional manipulation, you can empower yourself to set boundaries, prioritize self-care, and surround yourself with supportive connections that uplift and inspire you. Remember, you deserve friendships that nurture your growth, happiness, and authenticity, and it's okay to distance yourself from those that undermine your well-being.

Understanding Power Dynamics and Boundary Setting in Toxic Friendships

Toxic friendships are often characterized by imbalanced power dynamics and difficulties in setting and maintaining boundaries. In this chapter, we'll delve into the complexities of power dynamics in toxic friendships and explore the challenges of establishing boundaries, offering insights and strategies to empower you to navigate these relationships with confidence and self-respect.

Power Dynamics in Toxic Friendships:

1. Dominance and Control: In toxic friendships, one friend may exert dominance and control over the other, using manipulation, coercion, or intimidation to maintain power and influence.

2. Dependency and Submission: The dynamics of toxic friendships can foster a sense of dependency and submission, where one friend feels reliant on the other for validation, approval, or companionship.

3. Unequal Contribution: Toxic friendships may involve unequal contribution and reciprocity, with one friend consistently giving more than they receive, leading to feelings of resentment and imbalance.

4. Emotional Manipulation: Emotional manipulation is a common tool used in toxic friendships to exert power and control, often through guilt-tripping, gaslighting, or playing mind games.

5. Intimidation and Threats: Some toxic friendships may involve intimidation and threats as a means of maintaining power and dominance, leaving the other friend feeling fearful or powerless.

Challenges of Setting Boundaries:

1. Fear of Rejection: Setting boundaries in toxic friendships can evoke fear of rejection or abandonment from the friend, especially if they perceive it as a threat to their power or control.

2. Guilt and Obligation: Feelings of guilt and obligation may arise when attempting to set boundaries in toxic friendships, as the friend may use emotional manipulation or guilt-tripping to coerce compliance.

3. Boundary Violations: Toxic friends may disregard or violate boundaries, making it challenging to assert and maintain them effectively.

4. Manipulative Tactics: Manipulative tactics such as gaslighting or invalidation may undermine your confidence in setting boundaries, leading to self-doubt and confusion.

5. Lack of Self-Worth: Low self-esteem and feelings of unworthiness may hinder your ability to assert boundaries in toxic friendships, as you may fear repercussions or rejection if you stand up for yourself.

Navigating Power Dynamics and Boundary Setting:

1. Cultivate Self-Awareness: Reflect on the power dynamics within your friendship and how they impact your well-being. Recognize your own needs, values, and boundaries, and prioritize your self-respect and dignity.

2. Assertive Communication: Practice assertive communication techniques to clearly and confidently express your boundaries to your friend. Use "I" statements to assert your needs and feelings without blaming or accusing the other person.

3. Enforce Consequences: Be prepared to enforce consequences if your boundaries are disregarded or violated. Follow through with actions that protect your well-being and reinforce your boundaries.

4. Seek Support: Don't hesitate to seek support from trusted friends, family members, or mental health professionals who can offer guidance and validation as you navigate power dynamics and boundary setting in toxic friendships.

5. Know When to Let Go: Recognize when a friendship is too toxic or harmful to continue, and be willing to let go of relationships that undermine your well-being and self-respect. Focus on nurturing relationships that uplift and support you, and surround yourself with individuals who respect and honor your boundaries.

Navigating power dynamics and setting boundaries in toxic friendships is a challenging but essential aspect of self-care and self-respect. By cultivating self-awareness, practicing assertive communication, and seeking support, you can empower yourself to assert boundaries confidently and navigate toxic friendships with dignity and resilience. Remember, you deserve friendships that honor and respect your boundaries, and it's okay to distance yourself from those that undermine your well-being and self-worth.

Nurturing Healthy Connections: Strategies for Distance from Toxic Friends

Distancing yourself from toxic friends can be a difficult but necessary step towards prioritizing your well-being and fostering healthy relationships. In this chapter, we'll explore strategies to help you navigate the process of distancing yourself from toxic friends while nurturing and cultivating connections that uplift and support you.

Assessing the Friendship:

1. Reflect on the Relationship: Take time to reflect on the dynamics of your friendship and how it impacts your mental, emotional, and physical well-being. Consider whether the friendship is mutually beneficial and aligned with your values and priorities.

2. Identify Red Flags: Recognize signs of toxicity in the friendship, such as manipulation, betrayal, and emotional manipulation. Trust your instincts and acknowledge any feelings of discomfort or unease.

3. Assess Impact on Well-Being: Consider how the friendship affects your overall well-being, including your self-esteem, stress levels, and sense of fulfillment. Acknowledge any negative effects and prioritize your mental and emotional health.

Setting Boundaries:

1. Communicate Your Needs: Clearly communicate your boundaries and expectations to your friend, expressing your needs and concerns with honesty and compassion. Be firm and assertive in asserting your boundaries, and avoid apologizing or justifying your decision.

2. Limit Contact: Gradually reduce the frequency and intensity of your interactions with the toxic friend, setting boundaries around communication and socializing. Limiting contact can create space for introspection and self-care.

3. Enforce Consequences: Be prepared to enforce consequences if your boundaries are disregarded or violated. Follow through with actions that protect your well-being and reinforce your boundaries, even if it means ending the friendship.

Cultivating Healthy Relationships:

1. Identify Supportive Individuals: Surround yourself with supportive friends, family members, or mentors who validate your experiences and uplift you. Cultivate relationships with individuals who respect your boundaries and encourage your growth and well-being.

2. Invest in Self-Care: Prioritize self-care practices that nourish your mind, body, and soul, providing you with the strength and resilience to navigate the challenges of distancing from toxic friends.

3. Pursue Shared Interests: Engage in activities and hobbies that bring you joy and fulfillment, and seek out opportunities to connect with like-minded individuals who share your passions and values.

4. Foster Open Communication: Cultivate relationships built on open communication, honesty, and trust. Encourage dialogue and

mutual support, and be willing to listen and empathize with others' experiences.

5. Set Healthy Boundaries: Establish clear boundaries in your new relationships, communicating your needs and expectations with honesty and assertiveness. Prioritize relationships that respect and honor your boundaries, and distance yourself from individuals who disregard them.

Distancing yourself from toxic friends is a courageous act of self-care and self-respect, allowing you to create space for healthier, more fulfilling connections in your life. By assessing the friendship, setting boundaries, and cultivating healthy relationships, you can empower yourself to prioritize your well-being and surround yourself with individuals who uplift and support you on your journey of growth and healing. Remember, you deserve friendships that honor and respect your boundaries, and it's okay to prioritize your mental, emotional, and physical health above all else.

Chapter 4: Love and Toxicity: Escaping Abusive Partnerships

Understanding the Cycle of Abuse in Romantic Relationships

Abusive relationships are characterized by a cycle of behavior that can be difficult to recognize and break free from. In this chapter, we'll explore the cycle of abuse in romantic relationships, including the tactics used by abusive partners to exert control and manipulate their victims. Understanding this cycle is crucial for identifying abusive behavior and taking steps towards healing and safety.

The Cycle of Abuse:

1. Tension-Building Phase: The cycle typically begins with a tension-building phase, where minor conflicts, frustrations, or stressors escalate, leading to increased tension and anxiety in the relationship. During this phase, the victim may feel a sense of walking on eggshells or anticipating the abusive partner's anger or displeasure.

2. Explosive Incident: The tension eventually reaches a breaking point, resulting in an explosive incident of abuse. This can take various forms, including physical violence, verbal abuse, emotional manipulation, or sexual coercion. The abusive partner may justify their actions or blame the victim for provoking them.

3. Reconciliation and Apology: Following the abusive incident, the abusive partner may express remorse, apologize profusely, and promise to change their behavior. They may shower the victim with

affection, gifts, or gestures of reconciliation in an attempt to regain control and maintain the relationship.

4. Honeymoon Phase: The reconciliation phase is often followed by a honeymoon phase, where the relationship temporarily returns to a semblance of normalcy. The abusive partner may be attentive, loving, and affectionate, leading the victim to believe that the abuse was an isolated incident or that things will improve moving forward.

5. Repeat Cycle: Unfortunately, the cycle of abuse tends to repeat itself, with the tension-building phase leading once again to an explosive incident and the subsequent cycle of reconciliation and honeymoon phases. Over time, the abuse may escalate in frequency and severity, further entrenching the victim in the cycle.

Tactics Used by Abusive Partners:

1. Emotional Manipulation: Abusive partners often use emotional manipulation tactics to control and manipulate their victims. This can include gaslighting (distorting facts or reality to make the victim doubt their perceptions), guilt-tripping, or playing mind games.

2. Isolation: Abusive partners may isolate their victims from friends, family members, or support networks, making it difficult for them to seek help or escape the abusive relationship. This isolation serves to increase the victim's dependence on the abusive partner and maintain control.

3. Threats and Intimidation: Abusive partners may use threats, intimidation, or coercion to maintain power and control in the relationship. This can include threats of physical violence, harm to loved ones, or financial manipulation.

4. Economic Abuse: Economic abuse involves controlling or restricting the victim's access to financial resources, employment opportunities, or financial independence. This tactic can make it difficult for the victim to leave the abusive relationship or seek help.

5. Love-Bombing: Love-bombing is a manipulation tactic where the abusive partner showers the victim with excessive affection, attention, or gifts in an attempt to overwhelm and control them. This tactic can be used to lure the victim back into the relationship after an abusive incident.

Breaking the Cycle of Abuse:

1. Recognize the Signs: Educate yourself about the signs of abuse and recognize that you deserve to be treated with respect, dignity, and kindness in a relationship.

2. Reach Out for Support: Seek support from trusted friends, family members, or domestic violence hotlines if you're in an abusive relationship. You're not alone, and there are resources available to help you.

3. Develop a Safety Plan: Create a safety plan that outlines steps you can take to protect yourself in case of an emergency or escalation of abuse. This may include identifying safe places to go, packing a bag with essential items, and having a code word or signal to alert others of danger.

4. Seek Professional Help: Consider seeking therapy or counseling to process your experiences, build self-esteem and assertiveness, and develop coping strategies for dealing with the effects of abuse.

5. Leave the Relationship: If it's safe to do so, consider leaving the abusive relationship and seeking refuge in a safe environment. Remember that your safety and well-being are paramount, and you deserve to live a life free from abuse.

Understanding the cycle of abuse and the tactics used by abusive partners is essential for recognizing and breaking free from abusive relationships. By educating yourself about the signs of abuse, seeking support, developing a safety plan, and taking steps to leave the relationship, you can empower yourself to reclaim your life and build healthy, fulfilling relationships based on mutual respect, trust, and equality. Remember, you deserve to be treated with dignity and kindness, and there are resources available to help you break free from the cycle of abuse.

Recognizing Signs of Abuse in Relationships

Abuse can take many forms, and recognizing the signs is crucial for protecting yourself and seeking help. In this chapter, we'll explore the signs of emotional, verbal, and physical abuse in relationships, empowering you to identify red flags and take steps towards safety and healing.

Emotional Abuse:

1. Manipulation: Emotional abusers often use manipulation tactics such as gaslighting (making you doubt your perceptions or reality), guilt-tripping, or playing mind games to control and undermine your confidence.

2. Criticism and Insults: Constant criticism, insults, or belittling comments about your appearance, abilities, or worth are common in emotionally abusive relationships.

3. Isolation: Emotional abusers may isolate you from friends, family, or support networks, making you dependent on them for validation and companionship.

4. Control: Emotional abusers exert control over your behavior, decisions, or activities, dictating who you can see, what you can do, or where you can go.

Verbal Abuse:

1. Name-Calling: Verbal abusers may resort to name-calling, derogatory language, or insults to degrade and demean you.

2. Threats: Threats of violence, harm to yourself, loved ones, or pets, or threats of abandonment are common tactics used by verbal abusers to intimidate and control you.

3. Yelling or Screaming: Verbal abusers may escalate to yelling, screaming, or shouting matches to assert dominance and instill fear.

Physical Abuse:

1. Physical Violence: Physical abuse involves any form of physical harm or violence, including hitting, punching, kicking, slapping, or choking.

2. Property Damage: Physical abusers may destroy property or belongings as a form of intimidation or retaliation.

3. Restriction of Movement: Physical abusers may prevent you from leaving a room, home, or vehicle, or restrain you physically to exert control.

Recognizing the Signs:

1. Fear: If you feel afraid of your partner's reactions or behaviors, or if you walk on eggshells to avoid conflict, it may be a sign of abuse.

2. Low Self-Esteem: Constant criticism, insults, or belittling can erode your self-esteem and confidence, leaving you feeling worthless or inadequate.

3. Isolation: If you find yourself isolated from friends, family, or support networks, it may be a tactic used by your partner to control and manipulate you.

4. Excuses: Making excuses for your partner's behavior or justifying their actions to yourself or others may be a sign of abuse.

5. Physical Injuries: Unexplained bruises, cuts, or injuries, or frequent visits to the doctor or emergency room may indicate physical abuse.

Taking Action:

1. Trust Your Instincts: If something feels off or uncomfortable in your relationship, trust your instincts and seek help.

2. Reach Out for Support: Talk to a trusted friend, family member, or counselor about your concerns and experiences. You're not alone, and there are people who can help.

3. Safety Planning: Develop a safety plan that outlines steps you can take to protect yourself in case of an emergency or escalation of abuse. This may include identifying safe places to go, packing a bag with essential items, and having a code word or signal to alert others of danger.

4. Seek Professional Help: Consider seeking therapy or counseling to process your experiences, build self-esteem and assertiveness, and develop coping strategies for dealing with the effects of abuse.

5. Leave the Relationship: If it's safe to do so, consider leaving the abusive relationship and seeking refuge in a safe environment.

Remember that your safety and well-being are paramount, and you deserve to live a life free from abuse.

Recognizing the signs of emotional, verbal, and physical abuse is essential for protecting yourself and seeking help. By trusting your instincts, reaching out for support, and taking steps to prioritize your safety and well-being, you can break free from abusive relationships and create a life filled with respect, dignity, and love. Remember, you deserve to be treated with kindness and compassion, and there are resources available to help you on your journey to healing and recovery.

Developing an Exit Plan and Seeking Support

Leaving an abusive relationship can be a daunting and challenging process, but developing an exit plan and seeking support from trusted allies and resources is crucial for your safety and well-being. In this chapter, we'll explore strategies for creating an exit plan, identifying supportive allies, and accessing resources to help you navigate this difficult transition.

Developing an Exit Plan:

1. Assess Your Safety: Evaluate your safety and determine the level of risk involved in leaving the relationship. Consider factors such as the history of violence, access to weapons, and the potential for retaliation from your abuser.

2. Plan Your Exit: Develop a detailed exit plan that outlines steps you can take to leave the relationship safely. This may include securing important documents (e.g., ID, passport, financial records), packing a bag with essentials, and identifying a safe place to go.

3. Consider Legal Options: Familiarize yourself with your legal rights and options for obtaining protection orders, restraining orders, or other legal remedies to keep you safe from your abuser.

4. Financial Independence: Take steps to achieve financial independence and stability, such as opening a separate bank account,

securing employment or financial assistance, and creating a budget for living expenses.

5. Safety Planning: Create a safety plan that outlines strategies for protecting yourself in case of an emergency or escalation of abuse. This may include memorizing emergency contact numbers, establishing a code word or signal to alert others of danger, and practicing self-defense techniques if necessary.

Seeking Support from Trusted Allies:

1. Family and Friends: Reach out to trusted family members and friends who can offer emotional support, practical assistance, and a safe place to stay if needed.

2. Support Groups: Consider joining a support group for survivors of domestic violence or abuse, where you can connect with others who have experienced similar situations and access resources and guidance.

3. Therapists and Counselors: Seek support from therapists or counselors who specialize in trauma recovery and domestic violence. Therapy can provide a safe space to process your experiences, build coping skills, and develop strategies for healing and recovery.

4. Hotlines and Helplines: Utilize hotlines and helplines for domestic violence and abuse, where you can speak with trained advocates who can provide information, support, and referrals to local resources and shelters.

5. Legal Aid Organizations: Seek assistance from legal aid organizations or pro bono attorneys who can provide guidance and

representation in legal matters related to domestic violence, such as obtaining protection orders or navigating the legal system.

Accessing Resources:

1. Domestic Violence Shelters: Research domestic violence shelters or safe houses in your area where you can seek refuge and support while you plan your next steps.

2. Community Resources: Explore community resources and organizations that provide assistance to survivors of domestic violence, such as food banks, counseling services, and legal aid clinics.

3. Financial Assistance Programs: Investigate financial assistance programs for survivors of domestic violence, which may offer financial support for housing, transportation, childcare, or other essential needs.

4. Employment and Education Opportunities: Look for employment and education opportunities that can help you build financial independence and stability, such as job training programs, educational scholarships, or career counseling services.

Developing an exit plan and seeking support from trusted allies and resources is essential for leaving an abusive relationship safely and rebuilding your life. By assessing your safety, planning your exit, and accessing support from family, friends, therapists, and community organizations, you can take the first steps towards healing and recovery. Remember, you are not alone, and there are people and resources available to help you navigate this challenging journey. You deserve to live a life free from abuse and violence, and there is hope for a brighter future ahead.

Chapter 5: Setting Boundaries and Prioritizing Self-Care

Establishing Firm Boundaries for Self-Protection

Establishing firm boundaries is essential for protecting your mental, emotional, and physical well-being, especially in relationships where abuse or manipulation is present. In this chapter, we'll explore the importance of boundaries, how to establish them effectively, and why they are crucial for maintaining your autonomy, dignity, and safety.

Understanding Boundaries:

1. What Are Boundaries? Boundaries are limits or guidelines that define acceptable and unacceptable behavior, interactions, and expectations in relationships. They help safeguard your personal space, autonomy, and emotional well-being.

2. Types of Boundaries: Boundaries can be physical, emotional, or psychological. Physical boundaries involve protecting your personal space and physical safety, while emotional and psychological boundaries involve protecting your emotions, thoughts, and beliefs.

3. Importance of Boundaries: Boundaries are essential for maintaining healthy relationships, promoting self-respect and assertiveness, and preventing abuse, manipulation, or exploitation. They provide a framework for setting limits, expressing your needs, and asserting your rights.

Establishing Firm Boundaries:

1. Identify Your Needs: Reflect on your needs, values, and priorities in relationships. What behaviors or actions are acceptable to you, and what crosses the line? Clarify your boundaries to yourself before communicating them to others.

2. Communicate Assertively: Practice assertive communication techniques to express your boundaries clearly, directly, and respectfully. Use "I" statements to assert your needs and feelings without blaming or accusing the other person.

3. Be Consistent: Enforce your boundaries consistently and follow through with consequences if they are disregarded or violated. Consistency is key to establishing and maintaining firm boundaries.

4. Set Limits: Don't be afraid to set limits on your time, energy, and resources. It's okay to say no to requests or demands that compromise your well-being or values.

5. Trust Your Instincts: Trust your instincts and intuition when it comes to setting boundaries. If something feels off or uncomfortable in a relationship, listen to your gut and take action to protect yourself.

6. Practice Self-Care: Prioritize self-care practices that nourish your mental, emotional, and physical well-being. Taking care of yourself strengthens your resilience and reinforces your ability to maintain boundaries.

7. Seek Support: Surround yourself with supportive friends, family members, or professionals who respect and honor your boundaries. Seek guidance and validation from trusted allies as you navigate boundary-setting in relationships.

Protecting Your Well-Being:

1. Emotional Boundaries: Protect your emotional well-being by setting boundaries around how others treat you, speak to you, and interact with you. Communicate your feelings and needs assertively, and don't tolerate behavior that undermines your self-worth or dignity.

2. Physical Boundaries: Protect your physical safety and personal space by setting boundaries around physical touch, intimacy, and proximity. Assert your right to autonomy and bodily integrity, and don't hesitate to remove yourself from situations or relationships that compromise your safety.

3. Psychological Boundaries: Protect your thoughts, beliefs, and values by setting boundaries around what you're willing to tolerate or engage with mentally. Guard against manipulation, coercion, or gaslighting tactics that undermine your sense of reality or self-worth.

Establishing firm boundaries is a powerful act of self-care and self-respect, empowering you to protect your mental, emotional, and physical well-being in relationships. By identifying your needs, communicating assertively, and enforcing boundaries consistently, you can create healthy, respectful connections that honor and uplift you. Remember, you deserve to be treated with kindness, respect, and dignity, and it's okay to assert your boundaries to ensure your safety and well-being.

Learning to Say No and Assert Your Needs

L earning to say no and assert your needs is essential for maintaining healthy boundaries and fostering respectful relationships. In this chapter, we'll explore the importance of assertiveness, how to overcome barriers to saying no, and strategies for effectively communicating your needs in relationships.

The Importance of Assertiveness:

1. Assertiveness vs. Passivity and Aggression: Assertiveness is the ability to express your thoughts, feelings, and needs in a clear, direct, and respectful manner, without being passive or aggressive. It involves advocating for yourself while respecting the rights and boundaries of others.

2. Empowerment: Assertiveness empowers you to take control of your life, make choices that align with your values and priorities, and advocate for your well-being in relationships.

3. Boundary Setting: Assertiveness is closely linked to boundary setting, as it enables you to establish and maintain firm boundaries that protect your mental, emotional, and physical well-being.

Overcoming Barriers to Saying No:

1. Fear of Rejection: Fear of rejection or disapproval from others can make it difficult to say no. Recognize that it's okay to prioritize

your needs and well-being, even if it means disappointing others temporarily.

2. Guilt and Obligation: Feelings of guilt or obligation may arise when saying no, especially if you're accustomed to putting others' needs ahead of your own. Remember that taking care of yourself is not selfish but necessary for your health and happiness.

3. People-Pleasing Behavior: If you have a tendency to people-please or seek approval from others, it can be challenging to assert your needs or say no. Practice self-compassion and remind yourself that you deserve to prioritize your own needs and desires.

Strategies for Assertive Communication:

1. Use "I" Statements: Express your needs and feelings using "I" statements, such as "I feel overwhelmed when..." or "I need some time alone to recharge."

2. Be Direct and Specific: Clearly communicate your needs or boundaries in a direct and specific manner, avoiding ambiguity or beating around the bush.

3. Practice Active Listening: Listen actively to the other person's response, validate their perspective, and remain open to negotiation or compromise.

4. Set Limits: Set limits on what you're willing to tolerate or engage with, and don't hesitate to enforce consequences if your boundaries are disregarded.

5. Practice Self-Compassion: Be gentle with yourself as you navigate assertiveness in relationships. Remember that it's okay to make

mistakes or face challenges along the way, and every step towards assertiveness is a victory.

Asserting Your Needs in Relationships:

1. Romantic Relationships: Communicate your needs, preferences, and boundaries openly and honestly with your partner. Prioritize mutual respect, understanding, and compromise in your relationship.

2. Friendships: Assert your needs and boundaries in friendships by expressing your feelings and preferences assertively. Surround yourself with friends who respect and honor your boundaries.

3. Family Relationships: Communicate your needs and boundaries with family members in a calm and respectful manner. Set limits on interactions that are harmful or toxic, and prioritize your well-being above familial expectations.

Learning to say no and assert your needs is a transformative skill that empowers you to take control of your life, set healthy boundaries, and foster respectful relationships. By overcoming barriers to saying no, practicing assertive communication, and prioritizing your well-being in relationships, you can create connections that honor and uplift you. Remember, you deserve to be treated with kindness, respect, and dignity, and it's okay to assert your needs to ensure your happiness and fulfillment.

Practicing Self-Compassion and Prioritizing Self-Care for Healing

Healing from toxic relationships requires intentional self-care and self-compassion to nurture your mental, emotional, and physical well-being. In this chapter, we'll explore the importance of self-compassion, how to prioritize self-care practices, and strategies for reclaiming your sense of wholeness and healing after experiencing toxicity in relationships.

Understanding Self-Compassion:

1. Definition: Self-compassion involves treating yourself with kindness, understanding, and acceptance, especially during times of struggle, pain, or difficulty. It's about extending the same compassion and empathy to yourself that you would to a loved one in need.

2. Components: Self-compassion consists of three core components: self-kindness (being warm and understanding towards yourself), common humanity (recognizing that suffering is a universal human experience), and mindfulness (being present and nonjudgmental towards your thoughts and feelings).

3. Benefits: Practicing self-compassion has numerous benefits, including reducing feelings of shame, guilt, and self-criticism, enhancing resilience and coping skills, and promoting emotional well-being and self-esteem.

Prioritizing Self-Care Practices:

1. Physical Self-Care: Prioritize physical self-care practices such as getting adequate sleep, nourishing your body with nutritious foods, engaging in regular exercise or movement, and attending to any medical or health needs.

2. Emotional Self-Care: Nurture your emotional well-being by expressing your feelings, seeking support from trusted friends or therapists, practicing mindfulness or meditation, and engaging in activities that bring you joy and relaxation.

3. Mental Self-Care: Take care of your mental health by setting boundaries around negative self-talk or rumination, challenging unhelpful beliefs or thought patterns, engaging in creative outlets or hobbies, and seeking professional help if needed.

4. Social Self-Care: Cultivate supportive and nurturing relationships with friends, family members, or support groups who validate your experiences, offer empathy and understanding, and provide a sense of belonging and connection.

5. Spiritual Self-Care: Foster a sense of meaning, purpose, and connection to something greater than yourself through spiritual practices such as prayer, meditation, reflection, or engagement with nature.

Strategies for Healing:

1. Practice Forgiveness: Practice forgiveness towards yourself and others for past hurts and grievances. Let go of resentment and bitterness, and focus on moving forward with compassion and understanding.

2. Set Boundaries: Establish firm boundaries to protect yourself from further harm or toxicity in relationships. Communicate your needs and limits assertively, and enforce consequences if your boundaries are disregarded.

3. Seek Professional Help: Consider seeking therapy or counseling to process your experiences, heal from emotional wounds, and develop coping strategies for dealing with the effects of toxic relationships.

4. Engage in Healing Activities: Engage in activities or practices that promote healing and self-discovery, such as journaling, creative expression, spending time in nature, or participating in support groups for survivors of abuse or trauma.

5. Practice Gratitude: Cultivate a practice of gratitude by acknowledging and appreciating the positive aspects of your life, even in the midst of difficult times. Focus on moments of joy, connection, and resilience that bring meaning and fulfillment.

Practicing self-compassion and prioritizing self-care practices are essential for healing from toxic relationships and reclaiming your sense of wholeness and well-being. By treating yourself with kindness, understanding, and acceptance, and prioritizing your mental, emotional, and physical needs, you can nurture your resilience, foster self-empowerment, and create a life filled with love, joy, and fulfillment. Remember, you are worthy of love and compassion, and healing is possible with time, patience, and self-care.

Chapter 6: Forgiveness and Healing

Exploring the Complexities of Forgiveness in Toxic Relationships

Forgiveness is often seen as a pathway to healing and moving on from past hurts, but in the context of toxic relationships, it can be a complex and challenging process. In this chapter, we'll explore the intricacies of forgiveness, why it's not always straightforward in toxic relationships, and how to navigate this journey with compassion and self-awareness.

Understanding Forgiveness:

1. Definition: Forgiveness involves releasing feelings of resentment, anger, or vengeance towards someone who has wronged or hurt you. It's about letting go of negative emotions and finding peace within yourself, regardless of whether the other person apologizes or changes their behavior.

2. Components: Forgiveness consists of several components, including acknowledging the harm done, empathizing with the perpetrator's humanity, and making a conscious decision to release negative feelings and move forward.

3. Benefits: Forgiveness has been linked to numerous physical, mental, and emotional benefits, including reduced stress, improved mental health, increased resilience, and enhanced relationships.

Complexities of Forgiveness in Toxic Relationships:

1. Repeated Harm: In toxic relationships, forgiveness can be complicated by the pattern of repeated harm or abuse. It's challenging to forgive someone who continues to hurt you, especially if they show no remorse or willingness to change.

2. Power Dynamics: Forgiveness can be further complicated by power imbalances in toxic relationships, where the perpetrator holds control or authority over the victim. The pressure to forgive may come from societal norms or expectations, rather than genuine healing or reconciliation.

3. Emotional Safety: Prioritizing emotional safety is paramount in toxic relationships, and forgiveness should not come at the expense of your well-being. It's okay to set boundaries or distance yourself from the perpetrator if forgiveness feels unsafe or premature.

4. Trauma and Healing: In cases of severe abuse or trauma, forgiveness may not be necessary or even possible for healing to occur. Healing from trauma requires self-compassion, validation of your experiences, and support from trusted allies and professionals.

5. Self-Forgiveness: Forgiveness also involves extending compassion and understanding to yourself for any perceived shortcomings or mistakes. Self-forgiveness is an essential aspect of healing from toxic relationships and reclaiming your sense of worth and dignity.

Navigating the Journey of Forgiveness:

1. Validate Your Feelings: Validate your feelings of anger, resentment, or hurt towards the perpetrator. It's normal to experience a range of emotions in response to being mistreated or abused.

2. Set Boundaries: Set firm boundaries to protect yourself from further harm or toxicity in the relationship. Communicate your needs assertively and enforce consequences if your boundaries are disregarded.

3. Practice Self-Compassion: Practice self-compassion by treating yourself with kindness, understanding, and acceptance as you navigate the complexities of forgiveness. Be patient with yourself and honor your healing journey.

4. Seek Support: Seek support from trusted friends, family members, or therapists who can offer validation, empathy, and guidance as you navigate forgiveness and healing. Surround yourself with allies who respect and honor your experiences.

5. Release Expectations: Release expectations of how forgiveness should look or unfold. It's a deeply personal journey that may take time and reflection, and there's no one-size-fits-all approach.

Forgiveness is a complex and nuanced process, especially in the context of toxic relationships where harm or abuse has occurred. It's okay to acknowledge the complexities of forgiveness, honor your feelings, and prioritize your emotional safety and well-being above all else. Whether forgiveness ultimately comes or not, remember that healing is possible through self-compassion, self-awareness, and support from trusted allies. You deserve to reclaim your sense of peace, wholeness, and empowerment on your journey towards healing.

Embracing Forgiveness: A Journey Towards Liberation and Inner Peace

Forgiveness is a profound and transformative journey that can lead to liberation and inner peace. In this chapter, we'll explore the power of forgiveness, its profound impact on personal growth, and how embracing forgiveness can liberate you from the chains of resentment, anger, and pain.

The Power of Forgiveness:

1. Liberation from Resentment: Forgiveness liberates you from the burden of holding onto resentment and anger towards those who have wronged you. By releasing these negative emotions, you free yourself from their grip and open the door to healing and growth.

2. Inner Peace: Forgiveness cultivates inner peace by allowing you to let go of past hurts and find closure. It's about making peace with the past and embracing the present moment with a sense of acceptance and compassion.

3. Personal Growth: Forgiveness is a catalyst for personal growth and transformation. It requires courage, humility, and empathy, and it can lead to greater self-awareness, empathy, and resilience.

The Journey of Forgiveness:

1. Acknowledge the Pain: The journey of forgiveness begins with acknowledging the pain and hurt caused by others. It's important

to honor your feelings and experiences without judgment or suppression.

2. Shift in Perspective: Forgiveness involves shifting your perspective from one of victimhood to one of empowerment. Instead of seeing yourself as a passive victim of circumstances, you recognize your agency and ability to choose how you respond to adversity.

3. Cultivate Compassion: Cultivate compassion for yourself and others as you navigate the journey of forgiveness. Recognize the humanity and inherent worth of those who have hurt you, and extend empathy and understanding to yourself for any perceived shortcomings or mistakes.

4. Letting Go: Letting go is a key aspect of forgiveness. It's about releasing the need for revenge or retribution and surrendering to the flow of life with a sense of trust and acceptance.

5. Healing and Wholeness: Forgiveness is a pathway to healing and wholeness. As you release the weight of past grievances, you create space for love, joy, and fulfillment to enter your life.

Embracing Forgiveness:

1. Practice Self-Reflection: Reflect on your experiences, beliefs, and emotions surrounding forgiveness. Identify any barriers or resistance to forgiveness and explore ways to cultivate a mindset of openness and compassion.

2. Cultivate Gratitude: Cultivate a practice of gratitude for the lessons learned and the growth that has come from the experience of forgiveness. Focus on the blessings and opportunities that arise from embracing forgiveness.

3. Engage in Forgiveness Practices: Engage in forgiveness practices such as meditation, prayer, or journaling to deepen your understanding of forgiveness and cultivate a sense of peace and acceptance.

4. Seek Support: Seek support from trusted friends, family members, or therapists who can offer validation, empathy, and guidance as you navigate the journey of forgiveness. Surround yourself with allies who respect and honor your experiences.

5. Celebrate Your Growth: Celebrate your growth and progress on the journey of forgiveness. Recognize the courage and strength it takes to embrace forgiveness and honor yourself for your resilience and perseverance.

Embracing forgiveness is a profound and transformative journey that can lead to liberation and inner peace. By acknowledging the pain, cultivating compassion, and letting go of past grievances, you create space for healing, growth, and wholeness in your life. Remember that forgiveness is a personal journey, and it unfolds in its own time and in its own way. Trust in the process, and know that embracing forgiveness is a powerful act of self-love and empowerment.

Understanding Forgiveness Without Reconciliation and the Value of Remembering

Forgiveness is often misunderstood as synonymous with reconciliation, but the truth is that forgiveness does not always necessitate a return to the relationship or a restoration of trust. In this chapter, we'll explore the distinction between forgiveness and reconciliation, and why it's okay to move forward without forgetting the lessons learned from past experiences.

Forgiveness vs. Reconciliation:

1. Forgiveness: Forgiveness is a personal and internal process of releasing feelings of resentment, anger, or vengeance towards someone who has wronged you. It's about letting go of negative emotions and finding peace within yourself, regardless of the actions or behavior of the other person.

2. Reconciliation: Reconciliation, on the other hand, involves restoring a relationship or rebuilding trust with the person who has hurt you. It requires mutual effort, transparency, and commitment to addressing underlying issues and repairing the damage done to the relationship.

It's Okay to Move Forward Without Forgetting:

1. Learning from the Past: Moving forward without forgetting allows you to honor the lessons learned from past experiences. It's

an acknowledgment of the wisdom gained and the growth that has come from navigating challenges and adversity.

2. Setting Boundaries: Forgiveness without forgetting empowers you to set firm boundaries to protect yourself from further harm or toxicity in relationships. It's about recognizing your worth and prioritizing your well-being, even if it means maintaining distance from the person who has hurt you.

3. Honoring Your Truth: Remembering allows you to honor your truth and validate your experiences. It's a reminder that your feelings and perceptions are valid and worthy of acknowledgment, even if they differ from those of others involved.

4. Self-Preservation: Moving forward without forgetting is an act of self-preservation. It's about prioritizing your emotional safety and well-being above the pressure to reconcile or forget past transgressions.

Navigating the Journey of Forgiveness Without Reconciliation:

1. Acceptance: Accept that reconciliation may not be possible or healthy in every situation. It's okay to acknowledge the limitations of forgiveness and focus on your own healing and growth.

2. Set Boundaries: Set clear boundaries to protect yourself from further harm or toxicity in the relationship. Communicate your needs assertively and enforce consequences if your boundaries are disregarded.

3. Practice Self-Compassion: Practice self compassion as you navigate the complexities of forgiveness without reconciliation.

Treat yourself with kindness, understanding, and acceptance, and honor your healing journey.

4. Seek Support: Seek support from trusted friends, family members, or therapists who can offer validation, empathy, and guidance as you navigate forgiveness without reconciliation. Surround yourself with allies who respect and honor your experiences.

5. Focus on Healing: Focus on your healing and well-being as you move forward. Engage in self-care practices, cultivate gratitude, and celebrate your growth and resilience on the journey of forgiveness.

Understanding that forgiveness does not require reconciliation and that it's okay to move forward without forgetting is a powerful act of self-empowerment and self-preservation. By honoring your truth, setting boundaries, and prioritizing your well-being, you create space for healing, growth, and wholeness in your life. Remember that forgiveness is a deeply personal journey, and it's okay to navigate it in a way that feels authentic and empowering to you. Trust in your inner wisdom, and know that you deserve to live a life filled with peace, authenticity, and self-love.

Chapter 7: Moving Forward with Empowerment

Embracing the Journey of Self-Discovery and Personal Growth

Escaping toxic relationships is a courageous step towards reclaiming your autonomy, healing from past wounds, and rediscovering your sense of self. In this chapter, we'll explore the transformative journey of self-discovery and personal growth that unfolds after breaking free from toxic relationships.

The Journey of Self-Discovery:

1. Rediscovering Your Identity: Escaping toxic relationships provides an opportunity to reconnect with your authentic self and rediscover your passions, interests, and values that may have been overshadowed or suppressed.

2. Exploring Your Strengths: Embrace the journey of self-discovery by exploring your strengths, talents, and abilities. Recognize the resilience and courage it took to leave the toxic relationship and celebrate your inner strength.

3. Honoring Your Emotions: Allow yourself to feel and process a range of emotions, including grief, anger, and relief, as you navigate the aftermath of leaving a toxic relationship. Validate your experiences and honor the complexity of your emotions without judgment or self-criticism.

4. Cultivating Self-Compassion: Cultivate self-compassion by treating yourself with kindness, understanding, and acceptance as

you embark on the journey of self-discovery. Be gentle with yourself and acknowledge that healing takes time and patience.

5. Seeking Support: Surround yourself with supportive friends, family members, or therapists who can offer validation, empathy, and guidance as you navigate the journey of self-discovery. Seek out communities or support groups for survivors of abuse or trauma where you can connect with others who understand your experiences.

The Path to Personal Growth:

1. Healing from Past Wounds: Embrace the opportunity for healing and growth as you process and heal from past wounds inflicted by the toxic relationship. Engage in therapy, journaling, or creative expression to explore and release pent-up emotions and trauma.

2. Setting Boundaries: Set firm boundaries to protect yourself from further harm or toxicity in relationships. Communicate your needs assertively and enforce consequences if your boundaries are disregarded.

3. Cultivating Resilience: Cultivate resilience by embracing challenges as opportunities for growth and learning. Recognize the strength and resilience you've developed through surviving the toxic relationship, and trust in your ability to overcome adversity.

4. Pursuing Personal Goals: Set personal goals and aspirations that align with your values and passions. Whether it's pursuing a new career path, learning a new skill, or traveling to new places, embrace the freedom to pursue your dreams and aspirations.

5. Practicing Self-Care: Prioritize self-care practices that nourish your mental, emotional, and physical well-being. Engage in activities that bring you joy, relaxation, and fulfillment, such as exercise, meditation, spending time in nature, or connecting with loved ones.

Celebrating Your Growth:

1. Celebrate Your Progress: Celebrate your progress and milestones on the journey of self-discovery and personal growth. Recognize the courage and resilience it took to break free from the toxic relationship and honor your growth and progress along the way.

2. Embracing Your Authenticity: Embrace your authenticity and uniqueness as you rediscover and embrace your true self. Celebrate your individuality and honor the qualities and traits that make you who you are.

3. Gratitude and Reflection: Cultivate gratitude for the lessons learned and the growth that has come from navigating the challenges of escaping toxic relationships. Reflect on your journey with compassion and appreciation for how far you've come.

Embracing the journey of self-discovery and personal growth after escaping toxic relationships is a transformative and empowering process. By reconnecting with your authentic self, healing from past wounds, and embracing new opportunities for growth and fulfillment, you reclaim your power and create a life filled with purpose, authenticity, and self-love. Remember that you are worthy of love, happiness, and fulfillment, and trust in your ability to create the life you deserve.

Cultivating Healthy Relationships: Mutual Respect, Trust, and Authenticity

Healthy relationships are built on a foundation of mutual respect, trust, and authenticity. In this chapter, we'll explore the key principles and practices for cultivating healthy relationships that nurture your well-being and foster growth and connection.

The Importance of Healthy Relationships:

1. Emotional Well-being: Healthy relationships contribute to your emotional well-being by providing support, validation, and companionship. They offer a safe space to express yourself authentically and share your thoughts, feelings, and experiences.

2. Personal Growth: Healthy relationships encourage personal growth and self-discovery by challenging you to communicate effectively, set boundaries, and practice empathy and understanding. They foster an environment where you can learn, evolve, and become the best version of yourself.

3. Connection and Fulfillment: Healthy relationships enhance your sense of connection and fulfillment by fostering intimacy, trust, and genuine connection with others. They offer opportunities for shared experiences, joy, and laughter, and deepen your sense of belonging and purpose.

Key Principles for Cultivating Healthy Relationships:

1. Mutual Respect: Cultivate mutual respect by honoring each other's boundaries, opinions, and autonomy. Treat each other with kindness, dignity, and empathy, and avoid behaviors that undermine or disrespect the other person's worth or agency.

2. Trust: Build trust through honesty, transparency, and reliability in your interactions. Be trustworthy by following through on your commitments, keeping confidences, and communicating openly and authentically.

3. Communication: Foster open and honest communication by actively listening to each other, expressing your thoughts and feelings assertively, and seeking to understand each other's perspectives. Practice empathy and validation in your interactions, and avoid judgment or criticism.

4. Authenticity: Embrace authenticity by being true to yourself and expressing your thoughts, feelings, and values honestly and openly. Create a space where you and your partner feel safe to be vulnerable and authentic without fear of judgment or rejection.

5. Compromise and Collaboration: Practice compromise and collaboration in decision-making and problem-solving, seeking win-win solutions that honor both individuals' needs and preferences. Approach conflicts or disagreements with a spirit of cooperation and mutual understanding.

Practices for Cultivating Healthy Relationships:

1. Regular Check-Ins: Schedule regular check-ins with your partner to discuss your relationship, express appreciation, and address any

concerns or issues that arise. Use these check-ins as an opportunity to deepen your connection and strengthen your bond.

2. Quality Time Together: Make time for quality time together to nurture your connection and intimacy. Engage in activities that you both enjoy, whether it's going for a walk, cooking together, or simply spending time talking and connecting.

3. Support Each Other's Goals: Support each other's goals, aspirations, and passions by offering encouragement, validation, and assistance when needed. Celebrate each other's successes and milestones, and be a source of strength and encouragement during challenges.

4. Practice Forgiveness and Understanding: Practice forgiveness and understanding when conflicts or misunderstandings arise. Approach disagreements with empathy and a willingness to listen and understand each other's perspectives, and be open to finding resolutions that honor both individuals' needs.

5. Prioritize Self-Care: Prioritize self-care practices that nourish your mental, emotional, and physical well-being, both individually and as a couple. Take time for self-reflection, relaxation, and rejuvenation, and encourage your partner to do the same.

Cultivating healthy relationships built on mutual respect, trust, and authenticity is a transformative and rewarding journey. By embracing key principles such as mutual respect, trust, communication, and authenticity, and practicing habits that nurture connection and growth, you can create relationships that enrich your life and contribute to your overall well-being and happiness. Remember that healthy relationships require ongoing effort, patience, and commitment from both partners, but the rewards of deep connection, intimacy, and fulfillment are well worth the investment.

Finding Strength in Resilience and Empowering Others

Finding strength in your resilience and using your experiences to empower others is a powerful way to transform adversity into inspiration and connection. In this chapter, we'll explore how resilience can be a source of empowerment and how sharing your journey can inspire and uplift others.

The Power of Resilience:

1. Definition of Resilience: Resilience is the ability to bounce back from adversity, trauma, or setbacks and to adapt positively in the face of challenges. It involves drawing on inner strengths, resources, and support systems to overcome obstacles and thrive in the midst of adversity.

2. Cultivating Resilience: Resilience is cultivated through self-awareness, self-care, social support, and a growth mindset. It's about embracing challenges as opportunities for growth and learning, and recognizing that setbacks are not permanent obstacles but temporary setbacks.

3. Empowerment through Resilience: Resilience empowers you to take control of your life, overcome obstacles, and create positive change. It's a reminder of your inner strength, resourcefulness, and capacity to navigate life's ups and downs with courage and determination.

Using Your Experiences to Empower Others:

1. Sharing Your Story: Sharing your experiences of overcoming adversity can inspire and empower others who may be facing similar challenges. By being open and vulnerable about your struggles and triumphs, you create space for connection, empathy, and support.

2. Providing Hope and Encouragement: Your resilience serves as a beacon of hope and encouragement for others who may be feeling hopeless or defeated. By sharing how you've overcome adversity and found strength in resilience, you offer a message of hope and possibility.

3. Offering Support and Guidance: Use your experiences to offer support and guidance to others who are navigating similar challenges. Share practical tips, strategies, and resources that have helped you on your journey, and offer a listening ear and empathetic presence.

4. Advocating for Change: Use your voice and platform to advocate for change and raise awareness about issues related to resilience, mental health, and overcoming adversity. By speaking out and taking action, you contribute to a culture of empowerment and social change.

5. Creating Connection and Community: By sharing your experiences and connecting with others who have faced similar challenges, you create a sense of belonging and community. Together, you can provide mutual support, encouragement, and validation as you navigate life's ups and downs.

Finding Strength in Your Resilience:

1. Reflect on Your Journey: Take time to reflect on your journey of resilience and the challenges you've overcome. Celebrate your strengths, resilience, and growth, and acknowledge the lessons learned along the way.

2. Practice Self-Compassion: Practice self-compassion by treating yourself with kindness, understanding, and acceptance as you navigate the ups and downs of life. Be gentle with yourself and honor the resilience that resides within you.

3. Seek Support: Seek support from trusted friends, family members, or therapists who can offer validation, empathy, and guidance as you navigate the journey of resilience. Surround yourself with allies who respect and honor your experiences.

4. Cultivate Gratitude: Cultivate gratitude for the strength and resilience that have carried you through adversity. Focus on the blessings and opportunities that have emerged from your experiences, and express gratitude for the support and love that surrounds you.

Finding strength in your resilience and using your experiences to empower others is a powerful way to transform adversity into inspiration and connection. By sharing your journey, providing hope and encouragement, offering support and guidance, advocating for change, and creating connection and community, you can make a meaningful difference in the lives of others and contribute to a culture of empowerment and resilience. Remember that your resilience is a testament to your inner strength and courage, and by sharing your journey, you offer a beacon of hope and inspiration to others on their own path of healing and growth.

Epilogue: Embracing Your Liberation

Reflecting on Your Journey of Breaking Free from Toxic Relationships and Reclaiming Your Sense of Self-Worth

Reflecting on your journey of breaking free from toxic relationships is a powerful step towards reclaiming your sense of self-worth and empowerment. In this chapter, we'll explore the process of reflection, celebrate your resilience, and honor the growth and healing that has occurred along the way.

Acknowledging Your Courage:

1. Recognizing Your Strength: Acknowledge the courage it took to break free from toxic relationships and reclaim your autonomy. Celebrate your resilience, determination, and inner strength that propelled you forward in the face of adversity.

2. Honoring Your Journey: Reflect on the challenges you've overcome and the growth that has emerged from navigating the complexities of toxic relationships. Honor the lessons learned and the wisdom gained from your experiences.

3. Embracing Self-Compassion: Embrace self-compassion by treating yourself with kindness, understanding, and acceptance as you reflect on your journey. Be gentle with yourself and acknowledge the progress you've made, even if it's been a challenging road.

Reclaiming Your Sense of Self-Worth:

1. Recognizing Your Inherent Worth: Reclaim your sense of self-worth by recognizing your inherent value and dignity as a human being. Remind yourself that you are worthy of love, respect, and happiness, regardless of past experiences or relationships.

2. Letting Go of Shame and Guilt: Release any lingering feelings of shame or guilt associated with toxic relationships. Understand that you are not responsible for the actions or behavior of others, and forgive yourself for any perceived shortcomings or mistakes.

3. Setting Boundaries: Set firm boundaries to protect yourself from further harm or toxicity in relationships. Communicate your needs assertively and enforce consequences if your boundaries are disregarded.

4. Cultivating Self-Compassion: Cultivate self-compassion by treating yourself with kindness, understanding, and acceptance as you navigate the journey of reclaiming your sense of self-worth. Be patient with yourself and honor your healing journey.

5. Engaging in Self-Care: Prioritize self-care practices that nourish your mental, emotional, and physical well-being. Engage in activities that bring you joy, relaxation, and fulfillment, and surround yourself with supportive friends, family members, or therapists who can offer validation and encouragement.

Reflective Practices:

1. Journaling: Reflect on your journey through journaling, writing down your thoughts, feelings, and insights as you process your experiences. Use journal prompts to explore your emotions, identify patterns, and celebrate your progress.

2. Meditation: Practice meditation or mindfulness to cultivate inner peace and clarity as you reflect on your journey. Use guided meditations or mindfulness exercises to bring awareness to your thoughts and emotions without judgment.

3. Creative Expression: Express yourself creatively through art, music, or movement to explore your emotions and experiences in a nonverbal way. Use creative outlets as a form of self-expression and self-discovery.

4. Therapy or Counseling: Seek support from a therapist or counselor who can offer guidance and validation as you reflect on your journey of breaking free from toxic relationships. Therapy provides a safe space to explore your experiences, process your emotions, and develop coping strategies for moving forward.

Reflecting on your journey of breaking free from toxic relationships is a powerful and transformative process that allows you to reclaim your sense of self-worth and empowerment. By acknowledging your courage, honoring your growth, and embracing self-compassion, you can cultivate a deeper sense of authenticity, resilience, and well-being. Remember that healing is a journey, and reflection is an essential part of the process. Trust in your inner wisdom and resilience, and know that you are worthy of love, respect, and happiness.

Celebrating Your Newfound Freedom and Embracing a Life of Love, Joy, and Fulfillment

Breaking free from toxic relationships is a courageous act that opens the door to a life filled with love, joy, and fulfillment. In this chapter, we'll explore the journey of celebrating your newfound freedom, embracing the possibilities that lie ahead, and creating a life that honors your worth and happiness.

Embracing Your Freedom:

1. Acknowledging Your Liberation: Take a moment to acknowledge the liberation that comes with breaking free from toxic relationships. Celebrate the courage and resilience it took to reclaim your autonomy and well-being.

2. Letting Go of Limiting Beliefs: Release any limiting beliefs or doubts that may be holding you back from embracing your freedom fully. Recognize that you deserve to live a life of love, joy, and fulfillment, free from the constraints of toxic relationships.

3. Embracing Self-Expression: Embrace the freedom to express yourself authentically and pursue your passions and interests without inhibition. Allow yourself to explore new experiences, relationships, and opportunities that resonate with your true self.

4. Cultivating Independence: Cultivate independence by taking ownership of your life and decisions. Trust in your abilities and

intuition, and empower yourself to create the life you desire on your own terms.

Embracing the Possibilities:

1. Cultivating Love and Connection: Open your heart to love and connection by nurturing relationships that uplift and support you. Surround yourself with people who cherish and appreciate you for who you are, and cultivate deep and meaningful connections based on mutual respect and understanding.

2. Pursuing Joy and Fulfillment: Pursue activities and experiences that bring you joy, fulfillment, and a sense of purpose. Whether it's pursuing a hobby, traveling to new places, or giving back to your community, embrace the opportunities for growth and enrichment that come your way.

3. Embracing Growth and Learning: Embrace growth and learning as lifelong processes that enrich your life and expand your horizons. Stay curious and open-minded, and embrace challenges as opportunities for personal and spiritual growth.

4. Practicing Gratitude: Cultivate gratitude for the blessings and opportunities that surround you. Take time each day to reflect on the things you're grateful for, and savor the moments of joy, beauty, and connection that enrich your life.

5. Living Authentically: Live authentically by honoring your values, passions, and aspirations. Be true to yourself in all aspects of your life, and trust in the wisdom of your inner voice to guide you towards a life that aligns with your deepest desires and aspirations.

Celebrating Your Journey:

1. Reflect on Your Growth: Take time to reflect on the growth and transformation you've experienced since breaking free from toxic relationships. Celebrate the progress you've made and the resilience that has carried you through.

2. Express Gratitude: Express gratitude for the support and love that has helped you along the way. Thank those who have stood by your side and offered encouragement, validation, and empathy as you've navigated your journey.

3. Honor Your Strength: Honor the strength and courage it took to break free from toxic relationships and reclaim your sense of self-worth and empowerment. Recognize that you are a survivor and a warrior, capable of creating a life filled with love, joy, and fulfillment.

Celebrating your newfound freedom and embracing the possibilities of a life filled with love, joy, and fulfillment is a transformative journey that honors your worth and resilience. By embracing your freedom, cultivating love and connection, pursuing joy and fulfillment, and living authentically, you can create a life that reflects your true essence and brings you deep fulfillment and happiness. Remember that you are deserving of love, joy, and abundance, and trust in your ability to create the life you desire. Celebrate your journey, honor your strength, and embrace the possibilities that lie ahead with open arms and a grateful heart.

Breaking Free: Escaping Toxic Relationships with Family, Friends, and Partners

B reaking Free: Escaping Toxic Relationships with Family, Friends, and Partners is a compassionate and empowering guide for those seeking to liberate themselves from toxic relationships while embracing forgiveness as a tool for healing and growth. Through practical insights, personal anecdotes, and actionable strategies, this book empowers readers to prioritize their well-being and create a life filled with healthy, fulfilling relationships.

Understanding Toxic Relationships:

1. Recognizing Toxic Patterns: Learn to identify toxic behaviors and patterns in relationships, whether they're with family members, friends, or romantic partners. Understand how these dynamics impact your well-being and sense of self-worth.

2. Exploring the Roots of Toxicity: Dive deeper into the underlying factors that contribute to toxic relationships, such as codependency, insecurity, and unresolved trauma. Gain insight into how past experiences shape current relationship dynamics.

3. Setting Boundaries: Discover the importance of setting firm boundaries to protect yourself from further harm or toxicity. Learn practical strategies for asserting your needs and enforcing boundaries with compassion and assertiveness.

Embracing Forgiveness:

1. Understanding Forgiveness: Explore the transformative power of forgiveness as a tool for healing and growth. Learn how forgiveness can liberate you from the chains of resentment and anger, and create space for love and fulfillment.

2. Forgiving but Not Forgetting: Understand that forgiveness does not require reconciliation and that it's okay to move forward without forgetting. Embrace the journey of forgiveness while honoring the lessons learned from past experiences.

3. Embracing Self-Compassion: Cultivate self-compassion as you navigate the complexities of forgiveness and healing. Treat yourself with kindness, understanding, and acceptance as you prioritize your well-being.

Practical Strategies for Liberation:

1. Developing an Exit Plan: Create a roadmap for breaking free from toxic relationships, whether it's with family members, friends, or romantic partners. Develop practical strategies for disengaging from toxic dynamics while prioritizing your safety and well-being.

2. Seeking Support: Reach out to trusted allies, friends, family members, or therapists who can offer validation, empathy, and guidance as you navigate the journey of liberation. Surround yourself with a supportive community that respects and honors your experiences.

3. Prioritizing Self-Care: Prioritize self-care practices that nourish your mental, emotional, and physical well-being. Engage in activities

that bring you joy, relaxation, and fulfillment, and celebrate your resilience and courage along the way.

Creating Healthy, Fulfilling Relationships:

1. Cultivating Healthy Boundaries: Learn to cultivate healthy boundaries in your relationships, whether they're with family, friends, or romantic partners. Practice assertiveness and communication skills to honor your needs and preferences.

2. Nurturing Connection: Foster genuine connection and intimacy in your relationships by practicing empathy, active listening, and vulnerability. Create a safe space for authentic expression and mutual support.

3. Embracing Growth and Healing: Embrace the journey of growth and healing as you navigate the complexities of relationships. Recognize that healing is a process, and prioritize your well-being as you create a life filled with healthy, fulfilling relationships.

Breaking Free: Escaping Toxic Relationships with Family, Friends, and Partners offers a compassionate and empowering guide for those seeking to liberate themselves from toxic relationships while embracing forgiveness as a tool for healing and growth. Through practical insights, personal anecdotes, and actionable strategies, this book empowers readers to prioritize their well-being and create a life filled with healthy, fulfilling relationships. Remember that you are worthy of love, respect, and happiness, and trust in your ability to create the life you deserve.

www.ingramcontent.com/pod-product-compliance
Lightning Source LLC
Chambersburg PA
CBHW052144150726

48002CB00003B/1056